CONSTA
COUNTRY

FLATFORD AND THE RIVER STOUR

John Constable's Flatford

The unspoilt countryside along the valley of the River Stour is for ever associated with the work of John Constable, England's best-known landscape painter. Born in East Bergholt in 1776, he was the second son of a prosperous mill owner and corn merchant who owned two windmills and two watermills – Flatford and Dedham. Although the young John worked for his father for a time, his heart was not in it and he resisted pressure to take over the family business. At the relatively late age of twenty-three, Constable became a student at the Royal Academy where, by 1803, he was exhibiting regularly. Forced to support himself by painting portraits, it was as a landscape painter that he derived most satisfaction. Elected a full member of the Royal Academy in 1829, the year after the death of his beloved wife, Constable continued to live in Hampstead with his young family until his death in 1837. Much of his best-known work was painted within ten miles of his birthplace, and it is still possible to look at picturesque Flatford Mill or Willy Lott's Cottage and see the views which he painted scarcely altered.

Flatford Mill

Featuring in many of his paintings, including *The Haywain*, Willy Lott's Cottage attracts visitors from all over the world. Flatford Mill, which was built in 1733, is now owned by the National Trust and used as a Field Studies Centre. These scenes of cottage and church, meadow, stream and sky still delight the eye as they did when Constable said of them, "As long as I am able to hold a brush, I shall never cease to paint them."

Willy Lott's Cottage

Flatford Mill, 1817

Boat Building (detail), 1815

This famous view of boat building with its wealth of detail shows the boat dock, which is still visible today a little way downstream along the River Stour from Bridge Cottage.

Landscape: Boys Fishing, 1813

Today it is a tranquil waterway flanked by water meadows and shaded by poplars and willows, but once the River Stour was an important commercial thoroughfare. Barges regularly negotiated Flatford Lock, creating a fascinating scene for the young John Constable who captured the bustle and activity in several of his paintings. He spent long hours walking or riding through the lanes with his sketch-book, and later wrote, "I associate my careless boyhood with all that lies on the banks of the Stour; those scenes made me a painter."

Flatford Lock

The unspoiled countryside along the valley of the River Stour is for ever associated with the work of John Constable, and the Stour estuary which was so beloved of the artist has been designated an Area of Outstanding Natural Beauty. There are some superb walks in the vicinity of the river which is also an excellent area for bird-watching. Valley Farm, which stands opposite Flatford Mill and is now part of the Field Studies Centre, is one of the best-preserved medieval farmhouses in Suffolk.

Valley Farm   *Bridge Cottage*

View on the Stour near Dedham, 1822

Flatford Bridge, Dedham Church and Bridge Cottage are all clearly visible in this painting.

The Lock, 1824

East Bergholt

East Bergholt is a charming village situated on a ridge above the winding River Stour. In the Middle Ages the Stour Valley was a thriving centre of the wool trade, and there are several handsome houses in the village which were built by prosperous wool merchants. It was here that Constable was born on 11th June 1776, in a house built by his father near the church, and he later said that he loved "every stile and stump, and every lane in the village". In 1816 he married the granddaughter of the rector of St. Mary's Church at East Bergholt, *top right,* and both his parents are buried in the churchyard. Among the interesting monuments and memorials found in the church is one in honour of the artist's wife, Maria, and Constable himself is honoured in a stained glass memorial window. The tower of the 15th century church was never completed because the builders ran out of money and so the bells were hung in a wooden cage in the churchyard. Intended as a "temporary" arrangement, it still stands today, *top left.*

The Cornfield, 1826

One of Constable's best-loved paintings, *The Cornfield* is thought to depict Fen Bridge Lane, along which the artist walked to school, but in fact no church is visible from this lane.

Dedham

It is possible to walk beside the River Stour from Flatford Mill to the handsome country town of Dedham where John Constable attended the old grammar school. The road into the village passes many fine brick-and-plaster buildings, while the High Street boasts some elegant Georgian-fronted houses. Two early 16th century inns remain: The Sun, *bottom right,* once a busy coaching inn, and The Marlborough Head, which was originally the home and workshop of one of Dedham's prosperous clothiers and did not become an inn until 1702. St. Mary's Church, *centre,* is known for its outstanding carvings, and its tall tower is a prominent local landmark. It has featured in paintings, not only by Constable, but also by Sir Alfred Munnings who lived for many years in Dedham.

Dedham Lock and Mill, 1818

Dedham Mill, immortalised in Constable's painting, was where the artist worked as a young man.
An important mill which had its own wharves, granary and an adjacent cottage, Dedham was
the largest of the mills owned by his father, Golding Constable.

Dedham Vale

Dedham Vale, 1828

This superb painting, with its dramatic trees and sky, shows the full panorama of Dedham Vale viewed from Langham, to the west of the village. East Bergholt stands on the distant low hill to the left. Changes in the landscape can be seen by comparing this with Constable's painting of the same scene in 1802.